Life in the Sixt

by Mick Gowar

Contents

Section 1
Sci-Fi TV in the 1960s   2
Sporting Highlights   7

Section 2
Sixties' Fashions   12
Pop Music   18

Section 3
Civil Rights in the USA   22
The Space Race   27

Edinburgh Gate
Harlow, Essex

Sci-Fi TV in the 1960s

Science fiction (or sci-fi) shows were very popular on television in the 1960s. Some of the shows that started at this time were *Star Trek, Dr Who* and *Thunderbirds*. In the 1960s there was a real space race between America and Russia. Both countries wanted to be the first to conquer space. But on Earth, there was a race between the TV companies – to see who could make the most popular science fiction programme.

Star Trek

These are the famous words which began every programme:

Space: the final frontier. These are the voyages of the Starship Enterprise. Its five-year mission: to explore strange new worlds; to seek out new life and new civilisations; to boldly go where no man has gone before.

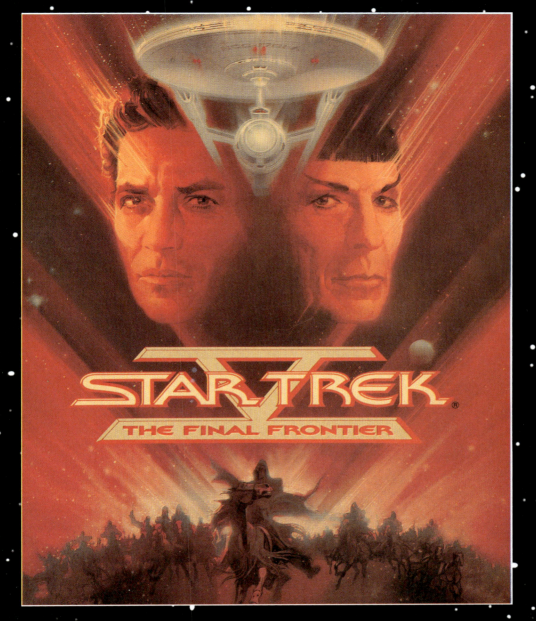

Star Trek *was so popular that films were made for the cinema*

The crew of the USS Enterprise visited many strange planets and met many strange aliens. Captain Kirk or one of the other crew members – maybe Mr Spock or Dr McCoy – often helped these aliens to solve problems. They would show the aliens how to stop fighting enemy nations and learn to live in peace.

Dr Who

One of the strangest sci-fi shows was *Dr Who*. The Doctor was not like other sci-fi heroes. He didn't just fight aliens from distant galaxies – he *was* an alien from a distant galaxy!

The Doctor was a Time Lord and could travel anywhere in space and time. His ship was called the TARDIS. The TARDIS always appeared as an old-fashioned police telephone box. Although it looked tiny from the outside, the inside of the TARDIS was enormous.

Dr Who and the Daleks in 1963

In his travels, the Doctor saved many planets from terrible dangers and enemies. The Doctor's worst enemies were the Daleks. The Daleks believed that they were the most superior race in the universe. Because they had very soft, weak bodies, the Daleks travelled everywhere in fighting machines. These machines looked rather like salt cellars. Their main weapons were a gun and something that looked like a sink plunger!

The Daleks showed no mercy. They killed any living thing that opposed them. When they were fighting, the Daleks would scream out their battle cry: "Exterminate! Exterminate!"

Millions of British children watched *Dr Who* from behind sofas and chairs because they were so frightened. But they never missed an episode!

Sporting Highlights

"I am the greatest!"

All through his career, the boxer Muhammad Ali boasted, "I am the greatest." Many sports writers have said that he was the greatest heavyweight boxer ever. Some have even said that he was the greatest athlete who has ever lived.

"I float like a butterfly and sting like a bee," was how Muhammad Ali described his style of fighting. He moved so fast that many boxers could only hit him a few times before he knocked them out.

Ali was also famous for being clever and quick-witted. He made up funny poems about his fights that predicted in which round he would knock his opponents out.

Muhammad Ali was a man with strong religious beliefs. He became a Muslim in 1964. In 1967 he refused to join the American army because of his religious beliefs. As a result, the organisation that ran world boxing said he could no longer be the World Heavyweight Champion. Many people were very pleased when he won the title back twice in the 1970s.

World Heavyweight Champion Muhammad Ali floors Sonny Liston in 1965

"They think it's all over ... it is now!"

Geoff Hurst scores England's third goal in the 1966 World Cup Final

In 1966 the football World Cup competition was played in England, so England was the host nation. Things started in the most embarrassing way for the host nation. Four months before the start of the competition, the cup was stolen from an exhibition. Luckily, it was found by a small dog called Pickles a few weeks later. It was wrapped in newspaper and hidden in a garden!

The final was between England and West Germany. West Germany scored after only 13 minutes. Six minutes later, the West Ham striker, Geoff Hurst, equalised. Then 12 minutes before the end of full-time, Martin Peters, another West Ham player, scored again. England was ahead 2–1. But just before the final whistle, Wolfgang Weber scored the equaliser for West Germany. The score was 2–2. The teams would have to play extra time.

Ten minutes into extra time, Geoff Hurst's shot hit the underside of the bar. It bounced down and then out of the goal. But had the ball gone over the goal line? Was it a goal? The Swiss referee wasn't sure. He asked his linesman. The linesman had no doubts. The referee blew his whistle: 3–2 to England.

Then, in the dying minutes of the game, the England Captain Bobby Moore hit a long pass for Geoff Hurst to chase. That was when the TV commentator said those famous words: "Some people are on the pitch, they think it's all over …" There was a pause as Geoff Hurst shot. The ball went into the roof of the goal. "… It is now!" added the commentator. England were World Champions.

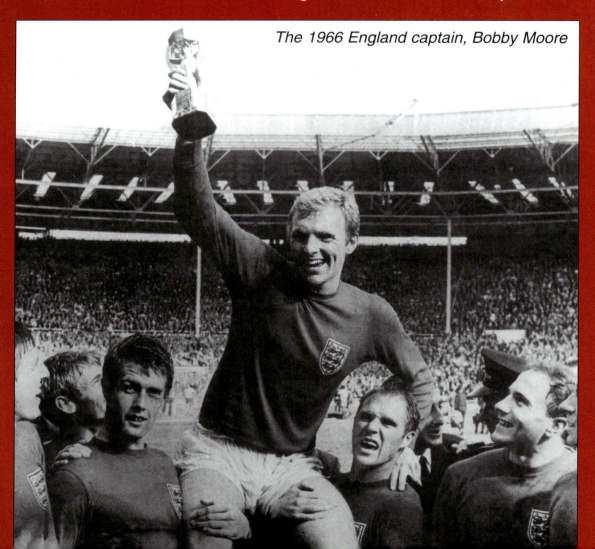

The 1966 England captain, Bobby Moore

Sixties' Fashions

In Britain in the 1950s many young people dressed, as they always had, in the same sort of clothes their parents wore. Young men wore suits and ties, or tweed sports jackets with grey trousers. Shirts were white, and teenage boys, like their fathers, wore hats when they went out.

Young women wore dresses like their mothers'. They also wore the same sort of underwear; even young girls wore girdles – a sort of elasticated corset.

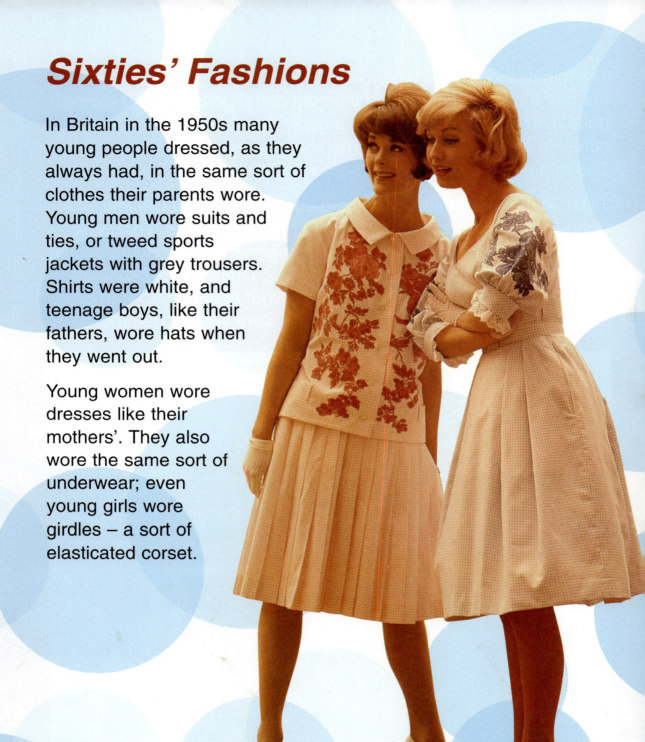

Upper-class youngsters had to follow even more rules. Girls wore different dresses for mornings, afternoons and evenings. And they always wore hats and gloves in public. Upper-class teenage boys were expected to change into evening clothes, even when having dinner at home. They would wear a dinner jacket and black tie for less formal events, and full evening dress with white bow ties and tail coats for formal parties, balls and dances.

This changed completely in the 1960s. Ordinary young people in Britain now had well-paid jobs, thanks to a booming economy. They wanted cheap clothes that were fun and – above all – wouldn't be worn by their parents.

The miniskirt

The best example of the new fashions for the young was the miniskirt or mini dress. Miniskirts were cut eight or nine inches above the knee. The miniskirt also meant the end of uncomfortable girdles, suspenders and stockings, which were replaced by tights and brightly coloured knickers.

Young designers like Mary Quant made and sold the first miniskirts. They were sold in clothes shops for young people which were given a special name: *boutiques*. The novelty of miniskirts wasn't just their length; they were made from new, cheap, washable fabrics like nylon and PVC. They were also printed with bold geometric patterns, many copied from the pop and op art paintings of artists like Bridget Riley.

Miniskirts horrified parents, teachers and vicars. In many schools, girls were forced to kneel on the ground to have their skirts measured. If they were too short, the girls were sent home and not allowed back to school until they were wearing a skirt that was long enough to be considered "respectable".

Shopping for clothes in Carnaby Street, London

Mods and Rockers

In the 1960s, clothes became an important way for young people to express who they thought they were. But in some cases, if you wore the "wrong" clothes you could end up in a fight.

By the mid 1960s, there were two distinct groups of young Britons: Mods and Rockers. Mods took their style from Italy. They drove Italian scooters, like Vespas and Lambrettas. Their clothes were smart and expensive – suits, Italian-designer casual clothes and handmade shoes. The music they liked was Afro-American dance music, like Tamla Motown and Soul, along with the new sounds from Jamaica – Ska and early Reggae.

The Rockers imitated American motorcycle gangs. They drove powerful motorbikes, dressed in denim and leather and liked traditional Rock 'n' Roll music. Mods and Rockers hated each other. During the summers of 1964 and 1965 they drove to seaside resorts like Brighton, Clacton and Margate. They fought running battles along the seafront with each other, and with the police who tried to stop them. As you can see from the newspapers, Mods and Rockers caused real problems.

Rockers

Pop Music

Many people think that the 60s was *the* decade of pop music. Performers such as the Beatles, the Rolling Stones, the Kinks, Bob Dylan, the Four Tops and Otis Redding made pop music in a lot of different styles.

Bob Dylan in concert

Many of the styles of 1960s' pop music were based on black American blues music, but performers and songwriters also took ideas from other types of music. They borrowed from folk music, political songs, British music hall songs and even classical music. By the end of the 1960s, pop music was no longer simply music for the young that was sneered at by anyone over 25. It was treated as a serious art form.

During the 1950s and 1960s many Americans were openly racist. At that time, radio stations for white audiences often refused to play records by black artists. Black music was only widely heard when white singers like Elvis Presley and Gene Vincent began recording black rhythm and blues music and calling it Rock 'n' Roll.

During the 1960s, as black Americans fought for and won their civil rights, black music and black artists started getting the recognition they deserved.

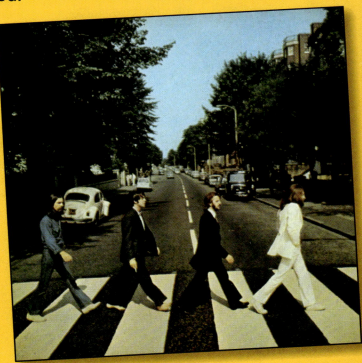

The Beatles in 1969

Motown

Motown Records produced some of the greatest dance music of the 1960s. Motown was founded by the black songwriter, producer and businessman Berry Gordy in Detroit in 1959. The name Motown is short for "Motor-town" because Detroit is also the home of the car manufacturer, General Motors.

The typical Motown group was a vocal group – either men or women – consisting of a lead singer and three or four backing singers. Many of the leading Motown artists had begun by singing in church. Later they seemed to have taken the idea of an evangelical preacher (the lead singer) supported by a choir (the backing singers) and applied it to performing love songs and dance music.

The Four Tops

The groups were backed by musicians who played drums and percussion, bass, guitar, keyboards and wind instruments. The musicians concentrated on playing the rhythms of a song. The piano and guitar didn't play the melody, but hammered out the rhythm by playing repeated chords. The melody was provided by the blended voices of the vocal group.

Groups such as the Supremes, the Four Tops, and Smokey Robinson and the Miracles were the star acts of Motown Records.

The Supremes

Civil Rights in the USA

Although laws had been passed in 1870 saying that every US citizen was equal, it wasn't until the 1960s that African Americans started to be treated fairly.

In 1960 in the Southern states of the US (the states which had allowed the owning of slaves until the Civil War) there were separate drinking fountains for whites and blacks, separate seating for whites and blacks in cinemas and restaurants, and separate schools and universities. Blacks were only allowed to sit in the back of buses and had to give up their seat if a white person wanted it.

Throughout the 1960s, extraordinarily brave black Americans campaigned, marched and protested to persuade the government to protect them from racist police, mayors and state governors who refused to treat black people equally. Several protesters were murdered by members of a racist secret society called the Ku Klux Klan. But the rightness of their cause, and the dignity and bravery with which the campaigners fought for their rights, convinced the US government to pass new laws. These laws would protect black Americans, give them equal access to health care and education and stop them being prevented from voting.

A group of college professors and black students are removed from a "whites only" waiting room and arrested in 1961

Martin Luther King

Martin Luther King was a Baptist minister and one of the main leaders of the Civil Rights Movement. Although he insisted on demonstrations being non-violent, he was often violently attacked by white racists. He had stones and other missiles thrown at him when he was leading demonstrations, and his home was bombed. In 1968 he was murdered by a gunman.

Martin Luther King was a wonderful speaker and a devout Christian. He would never respond violently no matter how violently he was treated by others. Much of the respect and support that the black Civil Rights Movement gained from Americans of all races was due to his leadership and example.

In 1963, he helped organise a march to Washington to persuade the government to pass new laws protecting black civil rights. On the steps of the Lincoln Memorial, Martin Luther King made one of his greatest speeches to the enormous crowd of marchers. It summed up many of his own beliefs and the aims of the Civil Rights Movement at that time.

Martin Luther King making his "I have a dream" speech in 1963

Here are some extracts from that speech:

> I have a dream that one day … sons of former slaves and the sons of former slave owners will be able to sit down together at the table of brotherhood.

> I have a dream that my four little children will one day live in a nation where they will not be judged by the colour of their skin but by the content of their character.

> I have a dream that one day … little black boys and black girls will be able to join hands with little white boys and white girls and walk together as sisters and brothers.

> I have a dream today … when all of God's children, black men and white men, Jews and Gentiles, Protestants and Catholics, will be able to join hands and sing in the words of the old Negro spiritual, "Free at last! Free at last! Thank God Almighty, we are free at last!"

Blacks march on Washington in 1963

The Space Race

The 1960s were part of a period known as the "Cold War". The Cold War began at the end of the Second World War and was a time of great rivalry between the USA and the Soviet Union, or USSR. The USSR was made up of Russia, Ukraine, Georgia and several Central Asian republics. The USA and the USSR each tried to build bigger and more terrifying weapons than the other, although there was never actually a full-scale war between these two "superpowers".

At the end of the Second World War, both superpowers had captured scientists and generals who had been working on the German rocket programmes. In October 1957, the USSR launched the first satellite into orbit. It was called Sputnik 1 and weighed 183 pounds. The following month they launched an even bigger satellite with a dog called Laika on board. Unfortunately for Laika, there were no plans for the satellite to return to Earth and she died in space.

America responded by launching a very small satellite of its own in 1958, but it was obvious that America was "behind" in the race to control space. Then in 1961 the new American President, John Kennedy, promised that the USA would put a man on the moon by the end of the decade. The American manned flights began with the Mercury programme which consisted of lone astronauts orbiting the Earth.

In 1963 the Apollo programme began. Each Apollo craft had a crew of three astronauts, and the aim of the project was to land two astronauts from an Apollo crew on the moon.

Apollo 11 lifts off at the Kennedy Space Centre to begin the first ever lunar landing mission

Astronaut Buzz Aldrin on the moon in 1969

On 20th July 1969, Neil Armstrong and Buzz Aldrin landed on the moon from Apollo 11. Neil Armstrong, the first man to step on to the moon, said as he stepped from the lunar spacecraft for the first time: "One small step for man, one giant leap for mankind."

The Apollo programme finished in 1972. Since then no one has landed on the moon. Between 1962 and 1972, the USA spent 5 billion dollars a year on the space programme – an enormous sum in those days.

Apollo 13

The most dramatic flight of the whole programme was Apollo 13. It was supposed to be the third moon landing, but several of the US TV channels weren't even broadcasting the live pictures of the astronauts in the spacecraft because the public were already getting bored with moon landings; they just didn't seem exciting enough. At one point someone at mission control even said to the crew of Apollo 13: "The spacecraft is in real good shape … we're bored to tears down here."

Nearly 56 hours into the flight, co-pilot Jack Swigert made his famous broadcast to mission control: "Houston, we've had a problem here." One of the two oxygen tanks on the service module had exploded, badly damaging the remaining tank. Apollo 13 was 200,000 miles from Earth and the normal supplies of oxygen, electricity, light and water had just been lost.

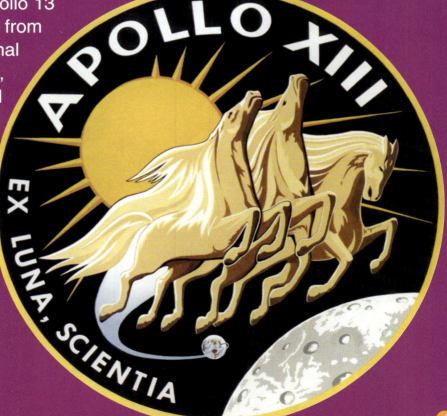

For more than three days the whole world watched and hoped as the astronauts flew their wrecked ship around the moon and, finally, back to Earth.

Some people said that it was bad luck to number the mission 13, because 13 was an unlucky number, so it was no wonder that there was almost a disaster. But maybe 13 turned out to be a lucky number, in fact, because, through their own skill and that of the people on the ground, the astronauts of Apollo 13 returned safely to Earth.

The astronauts land safely in the film Apollo 13